The Guitar Ninjas White Belt Book
Written by Michael Gumley

Copyright © 2023 Michael Gumley

All rights reserved. No part of this book may be reproduced in any form or by any electronic or mechanical means, including information storage and retrieval systems, without permission in writing from the publisher.

Editing by Michael Gumley
Front Cover Image by Michael Gumley
Book Layout & Design by Michael Gumley
All Musical Examples were written and arranged by the author unless otherwise credited.

Printed & Bound in Australia by GVP Education Publications
First Edition printing in February 2017
This Edition May 2023
Published by GVP Education Pty Ltd
Suite 2, 80 Raleigh St, Essendon, Vic, 3040

Visit www.GuitarNinjas.com.au for more!

Warning!

Unauthorised Photocopying, Recreation, or Distribution is Prohibited

www.GuitarNinjas.com.au

Contents

Introduction

White Belt Checklist 01
Introduction 02
Getting Started 03

Part 1 - Fundamental Skills

Lesson 1 - How To Pick 05
Lesson 2 - How To Fret 06
Lesson 3 - Reading Guitar Music 07
Lesson 4 - Notes Along The First String 08
Lesson 5 - Strumming 09
Lesson 6 - Picking Patterns 10
Lesson 7 - Picking Study 11
Lesson 8 - Strumming Study 12
Lesson 9 - Picking Pattern Study 13
Lesson 10 - The Major Scale 14
Lesson 11 - Skipping Notes 15
Lesson 12 - Changing Direction 16
Lesson 13 - Six String Picking Patterns 17
Lesson 14 - Speed Builder Exercises 18
Lesson 15 - Using Multiple Fingers 19
Lesson 16 - An Introduction To Riffs 20
Lesson 17 - Classic Rock Riffs 21
Lesson 18 - Modern Guitar Riffs 22
Lesson 19 - Learning The Notes 23

Part 2 - The Level-Up System

Lesson 20 - Introducing The Level-Up System 25
Lesson 21 - Level 1 - Bass Lines 29
Lesson 22 - Level 2 - Power Chords 30
Lesson 23 - Level 3 - One Finger Triads 31
Lesson 24 - An Introduction To Chord Progressions 32
Lesson 25 - Levelled Chord Progressions 33
Bonus Lesson - Play Along To Thousands Of Songs With The Four Chord Progression! 37

Part 3 - Misc

Tuning Your Guitar 38
Guitar Ninjas Practice Log 39

© Guitar Ninjas
The White Belt Book
www.GuitarNinjas.com.au

White Belt Checklist

This Book Belongs To

_____

This is what you need to attain your White Belt

Technique & Repertoire

- ☐ You have learned the Picking Skill and completed Lesson 4
- ☐ You have learned the Strumming Skill and completed Lesson 5
- ☐ You have learned the Picking Pattern and completed Lesson 6
- ☐ You have completed the Study Pieces in Lessons 7 - 13
- ☐ You have learned all 10 Guitar Riffs
- ☐ You have learned all 10 Chord Progressions and played them to Level 2
- ☐ You can hold the Guitar Pick correctly
- ☐ You are sitting with your Guitar correctly
- ☐ You are using the *'can of coke'* grip when fretting notes
- ☐ You are putting your fretting hand fingers right up against the edge of the frets

Knowledge

- ☐ You understand how to read Guitar Tab
- ☐ You understand how to read a Chord Diagram (pg 30)
- ☐ You understand how to read the timing values of Musical Notes (Guitar Workbook 1 pg 52)
- ☐ You can demonstrate the notes along String 6 (pg 29)
- ☐ You can play Power Chords
- ☐ You understand how to tune your own guitar

Attitude & Work Ethic

- ☐ You have brought your White Belt Book to your weekly guitar lesson for 3 weeks in a row
- ☐ You have created your Guitar Dojo Online account
- ☐ You have completed the White Belt Course on Guitar Dojo Online
- ☐ You have read/watched all four Guitar Practice Articles in the White Belt Course
- ☐ You have logged 10 days of practice using the Guitar Practice Log on page 39

Introduction

Congratulations on purchasing the Guitar Ninjas White Belt Book and taking the first crucial steps on your guitar-playing journey with us!

Learning guitar is a wonderful hobby that can lead to a lifetime of enjoyment for not only you but your friends and family too! Our little guide here will teach you everything you need to know about the guitar and all the skills you need in order to get started.

Over the next few pages, you are going to learn all of the basic skills and concepts that you need as a beginner. We structure our method in a way that allows you to grow in every area of your guitar playing simultaneously and most importantly, gets you playing songs and real music right away!

We're also a big advocate of teaching the underlying processes behind the skills, techniques and concepts that you need to learn. If we can show you the process of how to learn and practice skills in one context and you can take the process and apply it to new learning situations then you will make rapid progress in your guitar playing and musicianship skills.

We have divided this book into two sections:

1 - **Fundamental Skills** - Where you will learn the basic skills and how to quickly develop them along with some beginner riffs to get you started.

2 - **The Level Up System** - Where you will learn how to play along to any chord-based song using a simplified approach that you can build upon as your skills grow.

The third section of this book which contained special articles about learning guitar has been moved online to your Guitar Dojo Online account.

Getting Started With Guitar Ninjas

Access The Video Lesson Content

Although this is the White Belt Book you are in fact completing an entire course which takes you through the White Belt Level of Guitar Ninjas.

You can access video play-throughs for each concept and musical example in the book as well as exclusive insights and bonus lesson content via the **Guitar Dojo Online** virtual learning platform found at www.GuitarNinjas.com.au - Ask your teacher for help setting up your account.

Levelling Up

At the start of each method book you will find a checklist for all the skills and concepts that you need to learn in order to complete the book and level up. Simply tick off the items as you learn them or show them to your teacher and once you have ticked off all the list items you will level up and receive a certificate, a guitar strap reflective of your new level and the next book to start working on.

In the Guitar Ninjas Level-Up System you will progress from White, Yellow, Orange, Green, Blue, Purple, Red and Brown before becoming a Black Belt Guitar Ninja Master!

This Is A Workbook

This book is designed to be a hands-on workbook where you will complete challenges and tick off checklists. All students need their own copy of the book and should carry a pen or pencil so that they can tick off items as they go.

Part 1

Fundamentals

In the first part of this book, we will be introducing you to all of the fundamental skills, concepts and techniques that you need to play the guitar at a beginner level.

Start with Lesson 1 and work your way towards Lesson 18 in order to develop your fundamental skills and some basic repertoire.

Your teacher will help you in your lesson. You also have 24/7 access to the video play-throughs in the Guitar Dojo Online student portal.

Part 1

Lesson 1 - How To Pick

In this lesson you will learn your first fundamental skill: How to Pick.

A *Guitar Pick* or *Plectrum* is a small teardrop shaped piece of plastic used to help you pick on the guitar. We recommend that beginners get used to using a pick before exploring finger-style guitar, however if you don't have a guitar pick you can use the bottom edge of your thumb instead.

How To Pick

1. Start by holding the guitar pick between your thumb and first finger.
2. Point the pick back towards the guitar.
3. Bring the pick to the first string over the middle of the sound hole.
4. Pluck the string with a small but quick downward motion from your wrist.
5. Let the string ring out for several seconds
6. Repeat this 10 times on the first string (thinnest string)
7. Go on to repeat the motion 10 times on each of the 6 strings

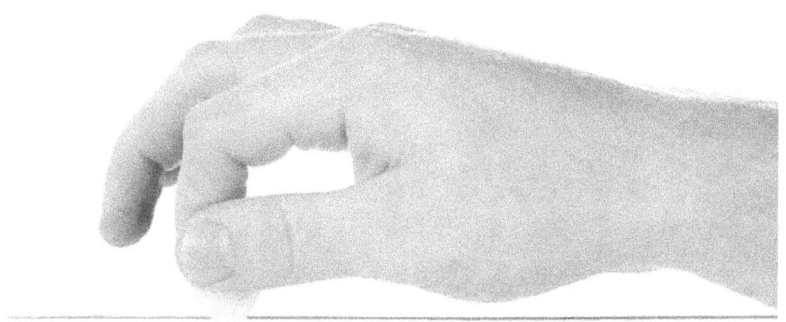

Tip: When picking, make sure you are gripping the pick firmly in the middle and pick with the same amount of movement as if you were holding a computer mouse and moving it about 2cm on the screen.

Lesson 2 - How To Fret Notes

In this lesson you will learn your second fundamental skill: Fretting.

A fret is a small metal bar embedded within the neck of the guitar. Putting your finger down behind a fret and squeezing shortens the length of the string and changes the sound that you hear. Think of each fret on the guitar like a key on a piano. The lower the fret, the lower the note, the higher the fret the higher the note.

How To Fret Notes

1. Hold your fretting hand as if you had an imaginary can of drink in it.
2. Rotate your hand so your thumb is pointing up towards the roof.
3. Place your thumb in the middle of the neck where the spine would be.
4. Curve your finger and bring the tip down right up near the edge of the first fret of the first string.
5. Squeeze hard enough to make the string presses against the wood
6. pluck the string with your picking hand and let it ring out for several seconds.
7. Now move to the 2nd fret and pick it, then the 3rd fret etc.
8. Play all the way to Fret 12 and back again!

Ex 1. How To Fret - Close To The Fret

Ex 2. How Not To Fret - In The Middle

Tip: Be as close to the fret as you can get without actually touching it. Don't be directly on top of the fret, and don't place it in the middle between two frets. Be as close as you can without actually touching the fret.

© Guitar Ninjas
The White Belt Book
www.GuitarNinjas.com.au

Lesson 3 - Reading Guitar Music

In this lesson you will learn how to read guitar music.

As guitarists we are lucky to have our own system of music notation called Guitar Tablature (or TAB for short). Guitar Tablature is a system of lines and numbers that correspond to our strings and the frets we need to play. Although reading standard music notation is a very important skill as beginners we want to start playing and having fun RIGHT NOW and can come back and learn to read music once we already know how to play.

Understanding Tablature

First you need to visualise the fretboard as if the guitar was laid out on a table in front of you with the thin string on top and the thick string on the bottom

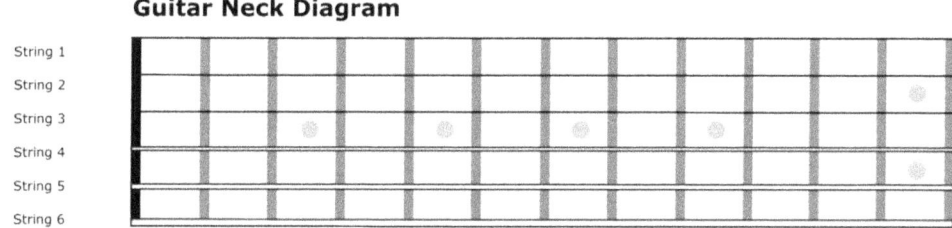

Secondly, you need to reduce the diagram to only include the 6 horizontal lines which represent the strings. Remember: Thin on top, thick on bottom.

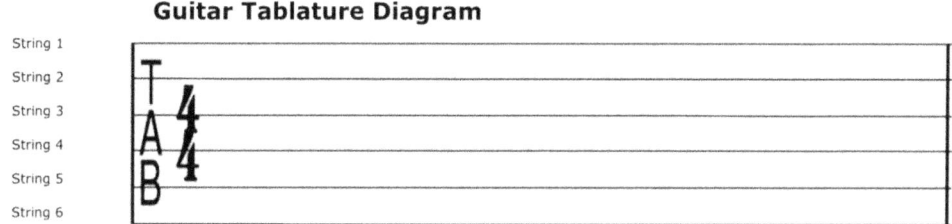

Try to first read, and then play the following examples:

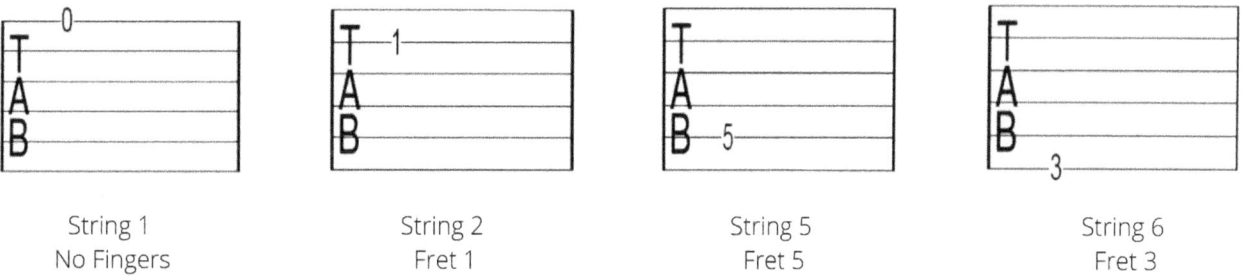

© Guitar Ninjas
The White Belt Book
www.GuitarNinjas.com.au

Lesson 4 - Notes Along The First String

In this lesson you will learn the notes along the first string and how to play them using the picking technique.

The first example below is the E Natural Minor scale. We'll outline the best way to learn and practice it below:

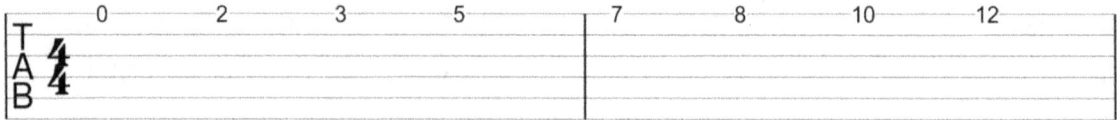

1. Say the first four numbers out loud three times.
2. Play the first four number three times.
3. Say the second four numbers out loud three times.
4. Play the second four number three times.
5. Say all eight numbers out loud three times.
6. Play all eight numbers three times.

We call this the '**Say It Three Times, Play It Three Times**' method. We have found that it is the best way to help you learn and memorise new information and to help you retain it long term. In the case of longer pieces of music you should do each indiviudal line of music three times each before putting the entire piece together.

Once you have learned a piece of music we recommend you try to play it in new ways to reinforce what you know and to challenge yourself. Try some of the following:

- Playing it backwards (from 12 to 0)
- Playing it 10 times in a row without any mistakes.
- Playing it using only upstrokes.
- Playing it while standing up.
- Playing it with your eyes shut.

How many can you do?

Lesson 5 - Strumming

In this lesson you will reinforce the E Natural Minor Scale you learned previously while also integrating it with a new technique called **Strumming**.

Strumming is when you play two or more strings at the same time using one single motion. Use the same motion as if you had just washed your hands and were flicking the water off.

We can identify strumming in Guitar Tab when the numbers are stacked up onto of eachother like the examples below:

   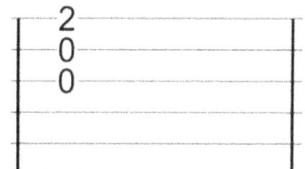

In the first example you can see three 0's stacked up on top of each other, this means they need to be played at the same time using the strum technique. In the second example we are fretting the 2nd fret of string 1 but still strumming the 2nd and 3rd string openly. Try playing the example below.

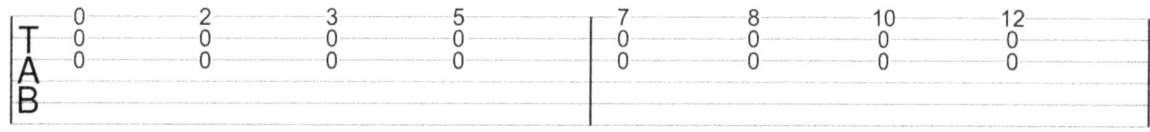

Hopefully you noticed that it was the same E Natural Minor Scale you learned in the previous lesson, but this time you are using strumming to include other strings. You should still

- Play it forwards three times.
- Play it backwards three times.
- Play it 10 times in a row without any mistakes.
- Play it while standing up.
- Play it with your eyes shut.

Lesson 6 - Picking Patterns

In this lesson you will you will learn how to combine your E Natural Minor Scale with picking patterns to create beautiful sounds on the guitar.

A **Picking Pattern** is simply a sequential order that you pick individual strings in that is repeated across one or several bars of music. Below is an example of what a picking pattern looks like in Guitar Tab

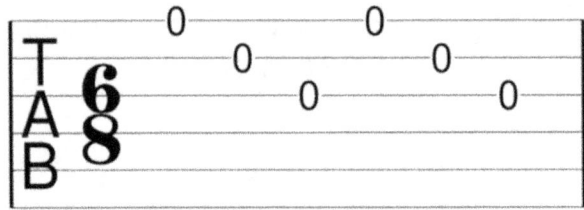

Unlike strumming where the numbers are stacked upon each other. We can see that we are still playing on multiple strings but individually in the order of the first string, then second, then third. Play this pattern over and over 20 times until you can do it smoothly.

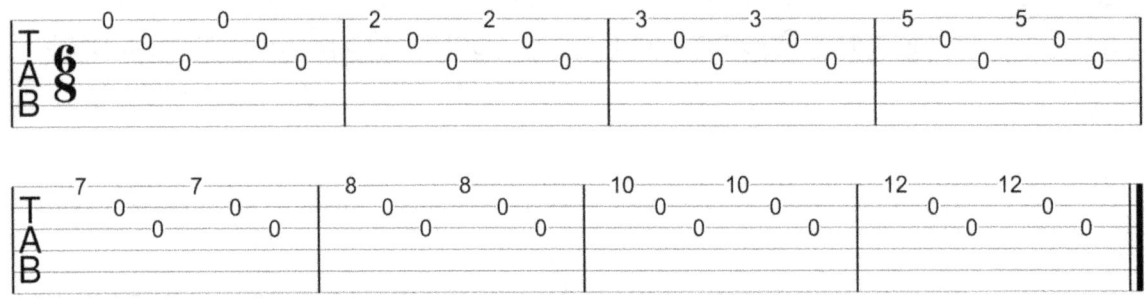

In the example above we are still playing our E natural minor scale, but are now applying a 6 note picking pattern to each note.

- Play the pattern twice on the open strings.
- Move your first finger to the 2nd fret on string one and play the same picking pattern.
- Keep moving along each note of the scale until you get to fret 12.
- Repeat this three times.

Congratulations! You have now learned all of your fundamental skills!

Lesson 7 - Picking Study

Here is a short study piece that uses our picking skill along the first string. This piece will reinforce your picking and fretting technique, and introduce you to learning larger pieces of music.

How to learn this piece.

- Say the first line three times, then play it three times.
- Say the second line three times, then play it three times.
- Say the third line three times, then play it three times.
- Say the fourth line three tines, then play it three times.
- Now play from the start of the piece to the end of the piece three times.

When you practice this way you are training your brain to remember the numbers and not be reliant of reading every single note. This will result in more of your attention going towards your fingers and making sure they are doing the right thing which will in lead to less mistakes and cleaner playing.

Of course, you can look up at the music for guidance whenever you need to.

Lesson 8 - Strumming Study

Here is a short study piece that uses our strumming skill combined with notes along the first string.

```
Line 1 (4/4):  12-0-0   10-0-0   8-0-0   7-0-0
Line 2:         8-0-0    7-0-0   5-0-0   3-0-0
Line 3:        12-0-0   10-0-0   8-0-0   7-0-0
Line 4:         5-0-0    3-0-0   2-0-0   0-0-0-0
```

How to Learn this Piece.

- Say the first line three times, then play it three times.
- Say the second line three times, then play it three times.
- Say the third line three times, then play it three times.
- Say the fourth line three tines, then play it three times.
- Now play from the start of the piece to the end of the piece three times.

Other Tips

Remember to let the notes ring out for four counts after each strum before you move onto the next note.

Be mindful that your pick doesn't come to rest on the third string in anticipation of your strum, this will mute the string.

Lesson 9 - Picking Pattern Study

Here is a short study piece that uses picking patterns along with notes on the first string.

Often the biggest challenge people have with picking pattern pieces is remembering the patterns and having to look between their hands each time they change string.

A great exercise to help overcome this is to focus on playing the pattern with your eyes shut. Play the pattern 3 times with your eyes open, then 3 times with your eyes shut. Open your eyes and play it another three times and then shut your eyes and try to get 5 times with your eyes shut. Open your eyes for 3 more times before trying to go 10 times in a row with your eyes shut. if you can do this, you won't need to look at your picking hand anymore.

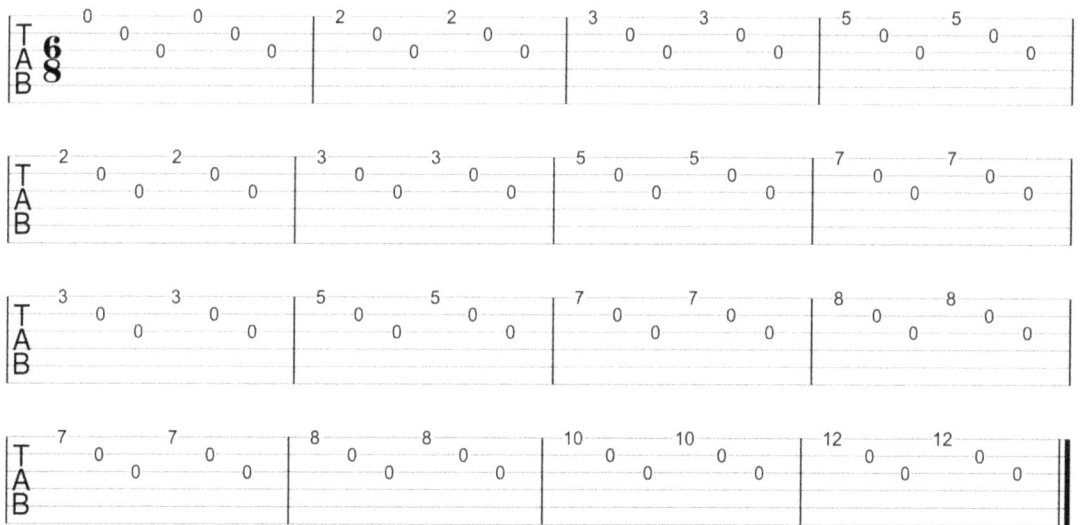

How to learn this piece.

- Say the first line three times, then play it three times.
- Say the second line three times, then play it three times.
- Say the third line three times, then play it three times.
- Say the fourth line three tines, then play it three times.
- Now play from the start of the piece to the end of the piece three times.

Lesson 10 - The Major Scale

Back In Lesson 5 you learned 8 notes along string number 1.

While you didn't know it at the time, you learned your very first scale - The Natural Minor Scale!

In this lesson you will learn the Major Scale, which is the foundation of all Western Music.

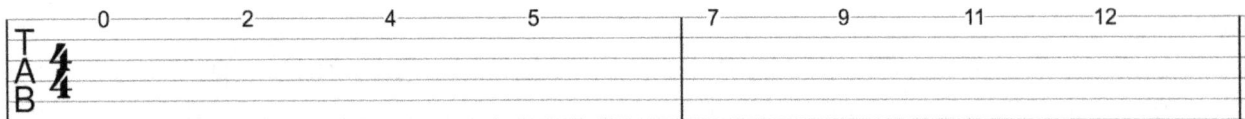

Use the **Say It Three Times, Play It Three Times** method to learn and practice the Major Scale along on string 1. Notice how it sounds and feels different to the minor scale you learned previously.

Major Scale Study Piece

Once you have learned the major scale above you can put it into practice with a brand-new study piece composed in the Key of E Major on string 1. Note that this piece uses several different rhythms so pay attention to which notes ring out for longer.

Tip: The pieces from here on will get longer and more challenging. To make learning easier break each line into individual bars, learn each part separately and then put them together before moving on to the next line.

Lesson 11 - Skipping Notes

Our next study piece will continue to use the E Major Scale on String 1.

This time we will be skipping notes in order to challenge your ability to change between notes smoothly.

You may wish to work on switching between two individual notes in isolation several times until it becomes smooth before you move on to the next notes.

This means that the 8 notes in the first line could be divided up into 4 chunks of two notes each, then two chunks of four notes, before putting the entire line together.

How to learn this piece.

- Say and play the first two notes three times each.
- Say and play the next two notes three times each.
- Say and play all four notes in the first bar three times each.
- Repeat steps 1-3 for the second bar on the first line.
- Put the entire first line together and play it three times.
- Repeat this process for all four lines before putting the entire piece together

Lesson 12 - Changing Direction

For this piece, we are returning to our Natural Minor Scale on String 1 which uses the notes 0 2 3 5 7 8 10 12.

We will be using a combination of note rhythms while playing melodies that ascend (go from low notes to high notes) and descend (high to low) in different directions.

Once again, learn the piece bar by bar before putting it all together.

Additional Levels

Try some of these additional levels to make the piece more challenging.

- Play the song as written on a single string
- Try playing the same notes but on a different string
- Try strumming the longer notes (include strings 2 & 3)
- Try strumming every note
- Try adding your own picking pattern to the piece
- Convert the piece from E Minor to E Major by changing the 3's to 4's and the 8's to 9's.

Lesson 13 - Six String Picking Patterns

Our final Study Piece includes the 6th string in the picking pattern and will sound a lot fuller as all the notes resonate with each other.

It's important to practice the picking pattern in isolation before attempting to apply it to the rest of the piece.

Remember, just say the number that changes in each bar (0 2 3 5, 7 5 8 7 etc) and apply the picking pattern.

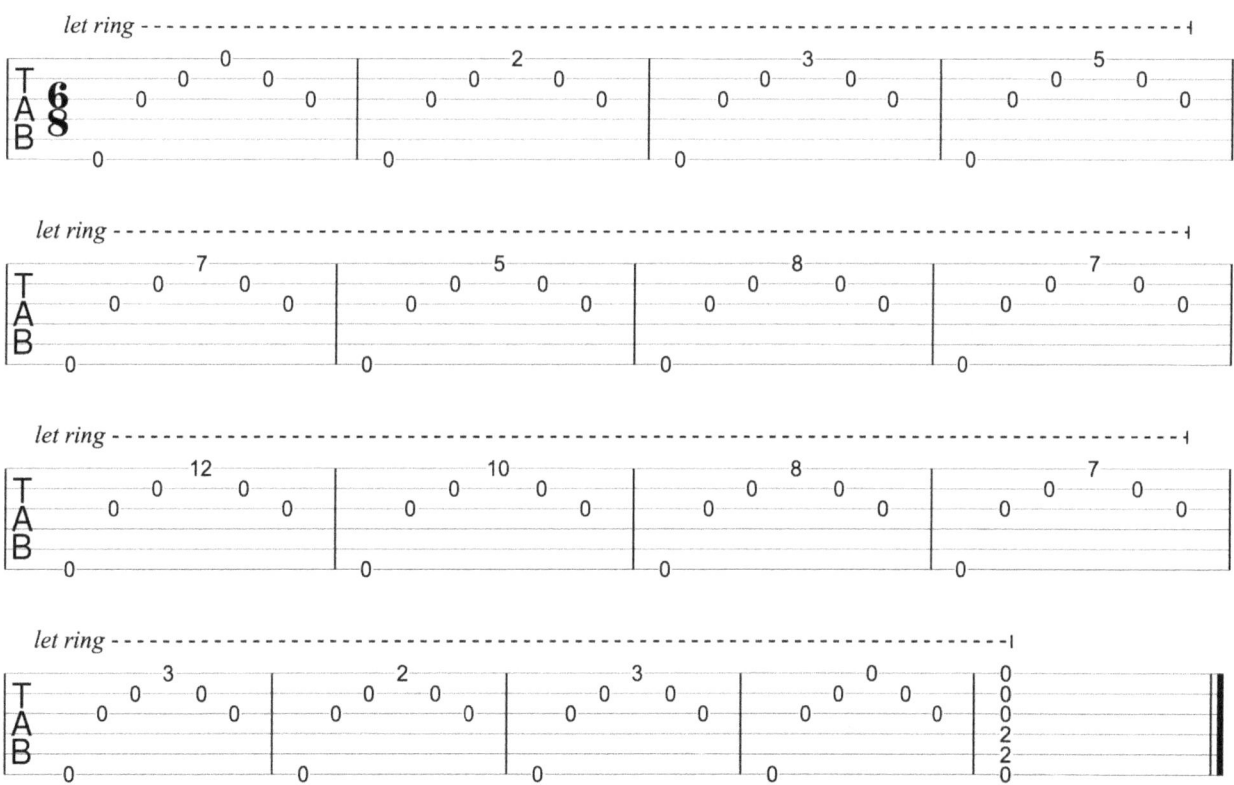

How To Learn This Piece

- Practice the picking pattern (6 3 2 1 2 3) in isolation until you can play it smoothly without mistakes
- Apply the picking pattern to the first four numbers (0 2 3 5) three times.
- Apply the picking pattern to the next four numbers (7 5 8 7) three times.
- Apply the picking pattern to the next four numbers (12 10 8 7) three times.
- Apply the picking pattern to the last four numbers (3 2 3 0) three times.
- Put it all together and finish with an Em chord strummed on all 6 strings.

Lesson 14 - Warmups

It's always a great idea to warm up your fingers before diving into rigorous guitar playing. In this lesson, you will learn 5 multi-finger warmup exercises that you can use to warm up while building your finger dexterity.

Aim to use your first finger on fret 1, your second finger on fret 2, your third finger on string 3 and your pinkie finger on fret 4. This will allow you to develop your ability to coordinate your fingers and have them do what you tell them to do.

Tick off boxes 1-5 for each individual example as you complete the challenges outlined below.

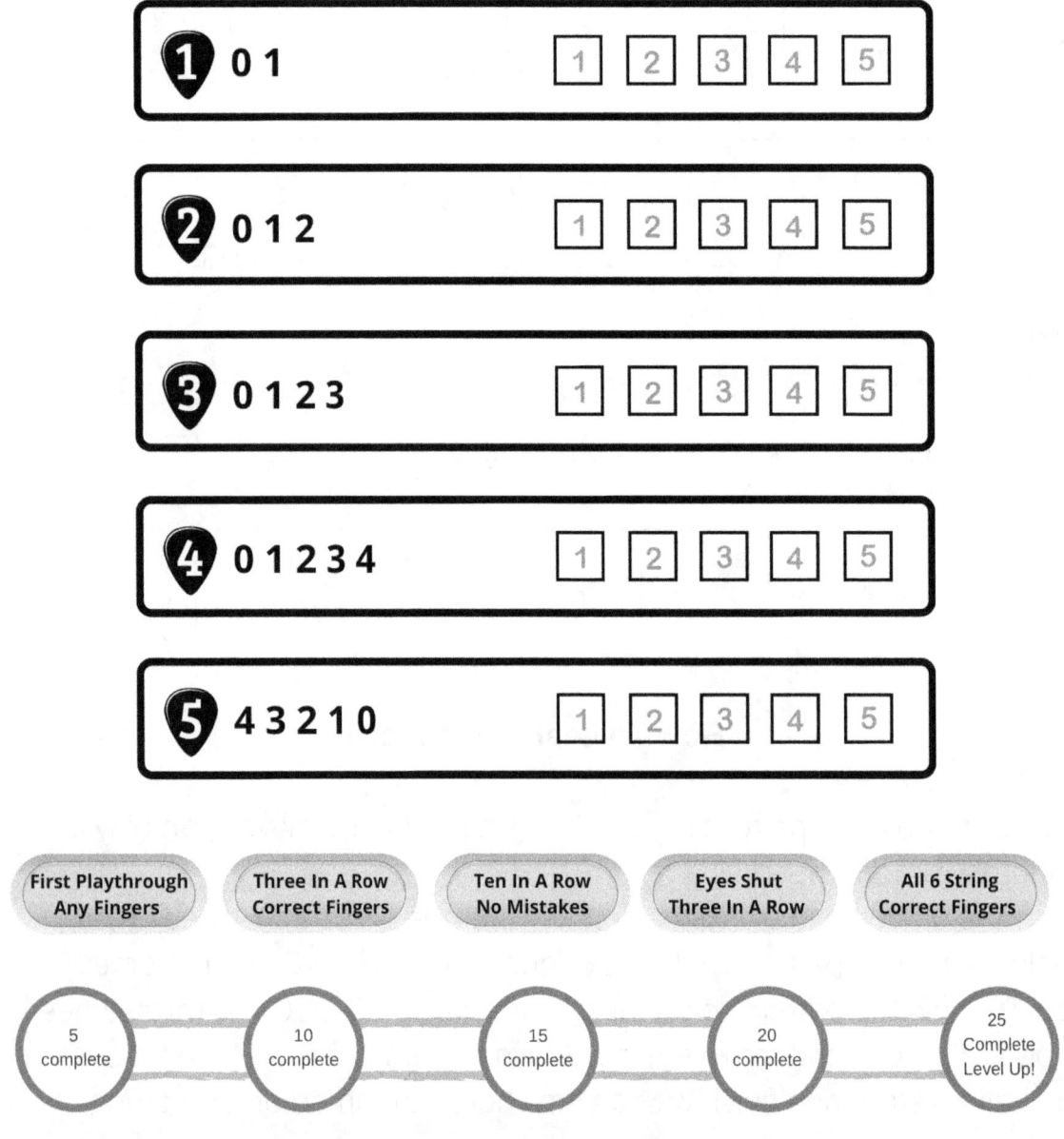

| First Playthrough Any Fingers | Three In A Row Correct Fingers | Ten In A Row No Mistakes | Eyes Shut Three In A Row | All 6 String Correct Fingers |

- 5 complete
- 10 complete
- 15 complete
- 20 complete
- 25 Complete Level Up!

© Guitar Ninjas
The White Belt Book
www.GuitarNinjas.com.au

Lesson 15 - Using Multiple Fingers

When it comes to using multiple fingers we can employ three patterns to help us find which fingers to match to the notes being played.

- The Green Pattern is a 4 fret stretch that we play with fingers 1 - 2 - 4
- The Blue Pattern is a 4 fret stretch that we play with fingers 1 - 3 - 4
- The Red Pattern is a 5 fret stretch that we play with fingers 1 - 2 - 4

In all 3 cases, put your first finger on the lowest note, your pinkie finger on the highest note, and assign your second or third finger to the note in the middle depending on which colour it is. Try the patterns with the exercises below.

1. 2 3 5 3 | 1 | 2 | 3 | 4 | 5 |

2. 3 5 7 5 | 1 | 2 | 3 | 4 | 5 |

3. 5 7 8 7 | 1 | 2 | 3 | 4 | 5 |

4. 7 8 10 8 | 1 | 2 | 3 | 4 | 5 |

5. 8 10 12 10 | 1 | 2 | 3 | 4 | 5 |

| First Playthrough Any Fingers | Three In A Row Correct Fingers | Ten In A Row No Mistakes | Eyes Shut Three In A Row | All 6 String Correct Fingers |

| 5 complete | 10 complete | 15 complete | 20 complete | 25 Complete Level Up! |

Lesson 16 - An Introduction To Riffs

A **riff** is a short, repeated pattern of music usually played on the lower strings of the guitar. It is often associated with the most memorable part of the song. If I tell you to think of '*Smoke on the Water*' or "*Back In Black*' chances are you can already hear the riff in your head.

We like to teach our students riffs for 3 reasons:

- They are easy and lots of fun to play
- They help you develop your timing and rhythm skills
- You can show them off to people straight away.

To learn riffs, we combine the say it three times, play it three times learning process with our fret numbers and clapping in order to get the feel for the riff before playing it on the guitar.

Let's take a look at the riff to *Hit The Road Jack* below:

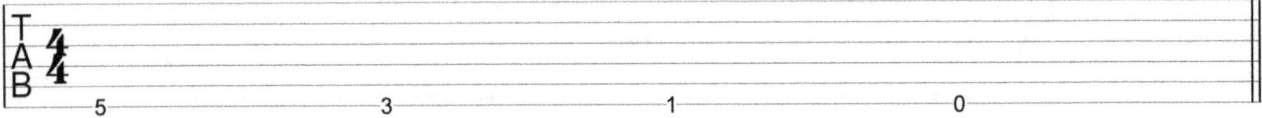

A quick look at the riff above tells us that we are playing on string 6 and that we are only playing four notes: fret 5, fret 3, fret 1 and the open string.

How You Should Learn This Riff

- Listen to the song so you know what the riff sounds like
- Clap along to the riff to internalise the rhythm.
- Clap along to the riff while saying the fret numbers aloud to memorise them.
- Play the riff on your guitar.

By definition, Riffs are repeated patterns, so make sure you play the riff you are working on at least 10 times in a row before you move on.

Learning Tip: More complex riffs can be broken into chunks and pieced together like any other musical example

Lesson 17 - Classic Rock Riffs

Here are 5 easy riffs to get you started. Don't forget to use the process we outlined on the previous page to help you learn and master each riff.

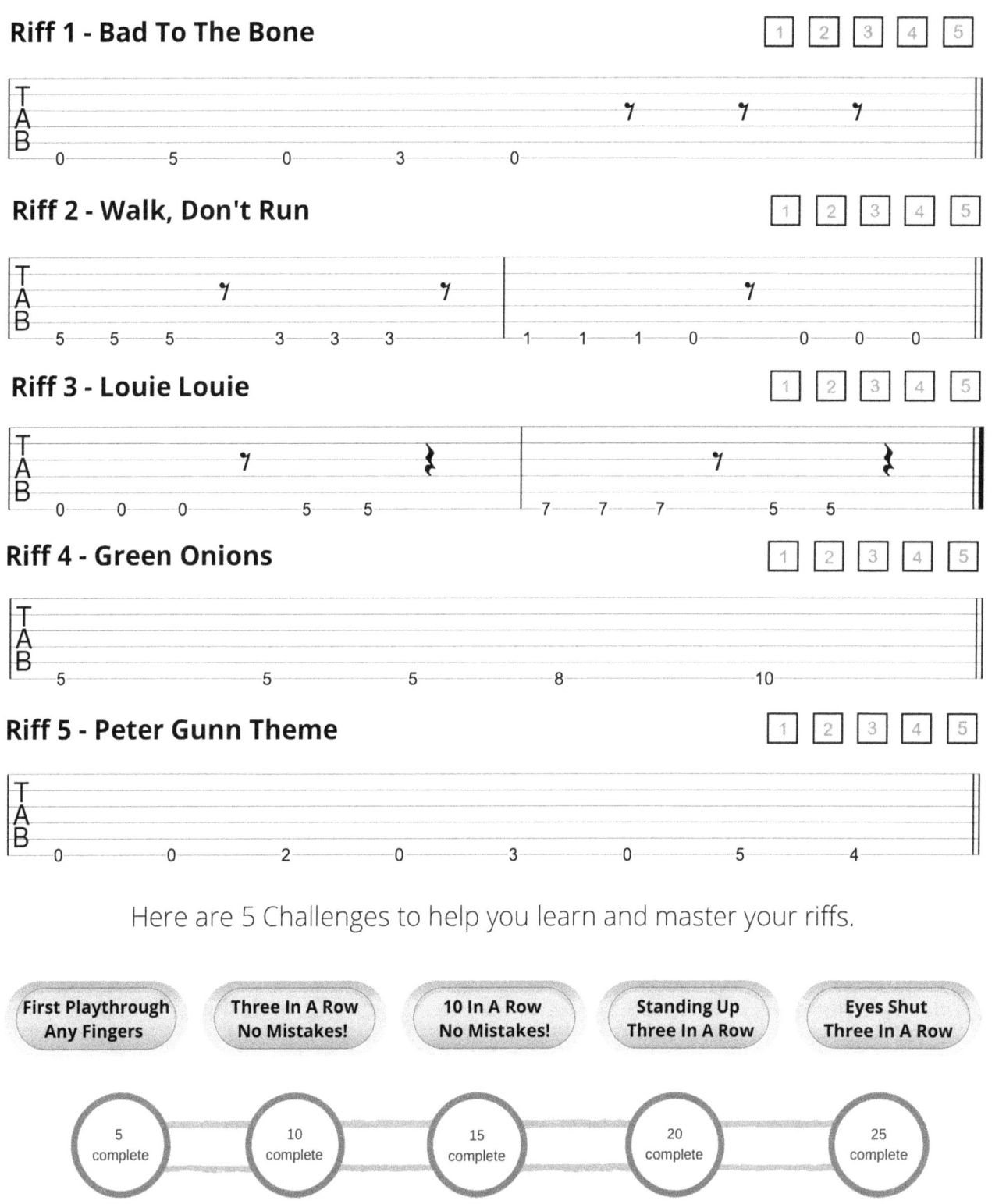

Here are 5 Challenges to help you learn and master your riffs.

Lesson 18 - Easy Modern Riffs

Here are 5 more contemporary riffs that you're bound to recognise.

Riff 1 - Believer

| 1 | 2 | 3 | 4 | 5 |

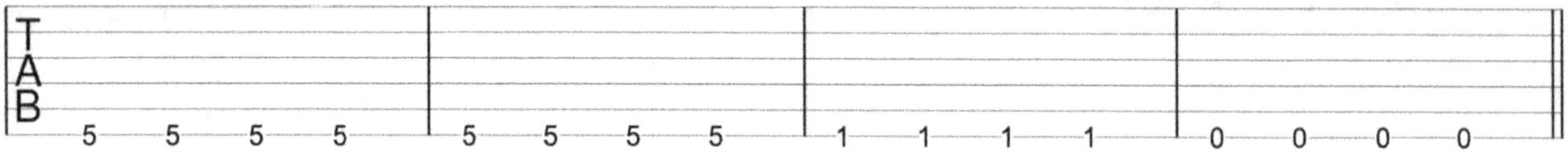

```
T|---------------|---------------|---------------|---------------|
A|---------------|---------------|---------------|---------------|
B|-5-5-5---5-----|-5-5-5---5-----|-1-1-1---1-----|-0-0-0---0-----|
```

Riff 2 - Shake It Off

| 1 | 2 | 3 | 4 | 5 |

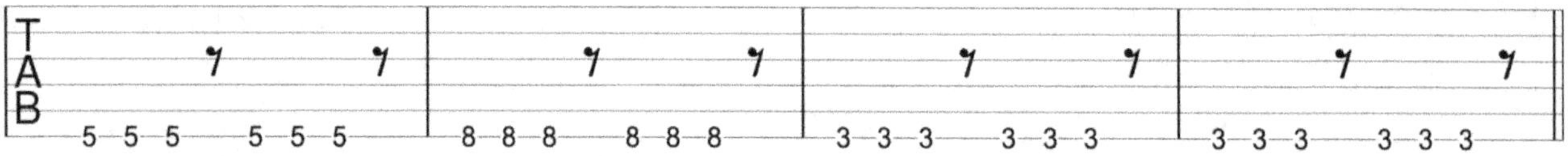

```
T|----7-----7----|----7-----7----|----7-----7----|----7-----7----|
A|---------------|---------------|---------------|---------------|
B|-5-5-5---5-5-5-|-8-8-8---8-8-8-|-3-3-3---3-3-3-|-3-3-3---3-3-3-|
```

Riff 3 - Love Yourself

| 1 | 2 | 3 | 4 | 5 |

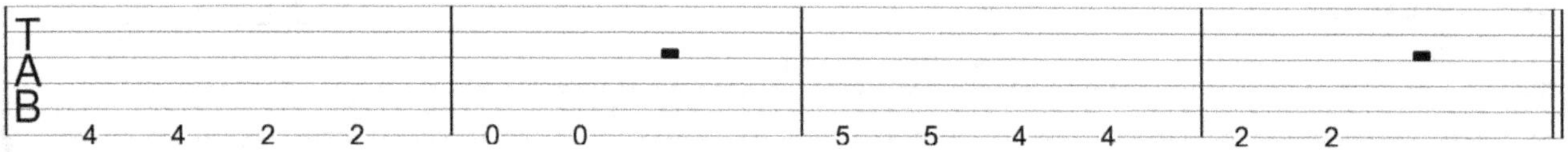

```
T|---------------|---------------|---------------|---------------|
A|-4---4---2---2-|-0---0---------|-5---5---4---4-|-2---2---------|
B|---------------|---------------|---------------|---------------|
```

Riff 4 - Uptown Funk

| 1 | 2 | 3 | 4 | 5 |

```
T|---------------|---------------|---------------|---------------|
A|---------------|---------------|---------------|---------------|
B|-5-------5-----|-10---8---5----|-10---8---4----|---------------|
```

Riff 5 - Castle On The Hill

| 1 | 2 | 3 | 4 | 5 |

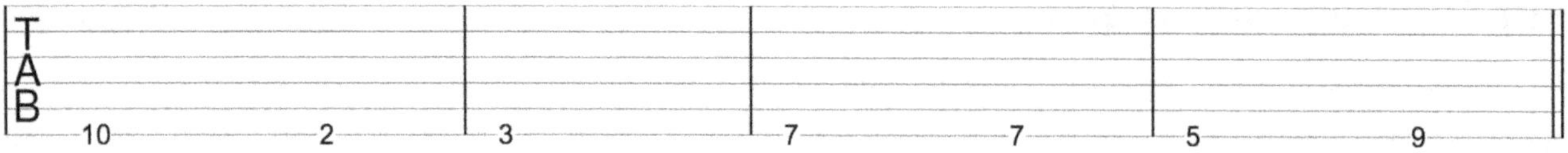

```
T|---------------|---------------|---------------|---------------|
A|---------------|---------------|---------------|---------------|
B|-10---2---3----|-7-------7-----|-5-------9-----|---------------|
```

Tip: In addition to the regular riff challenges below, you can also try playing your riffs using Power Chords.

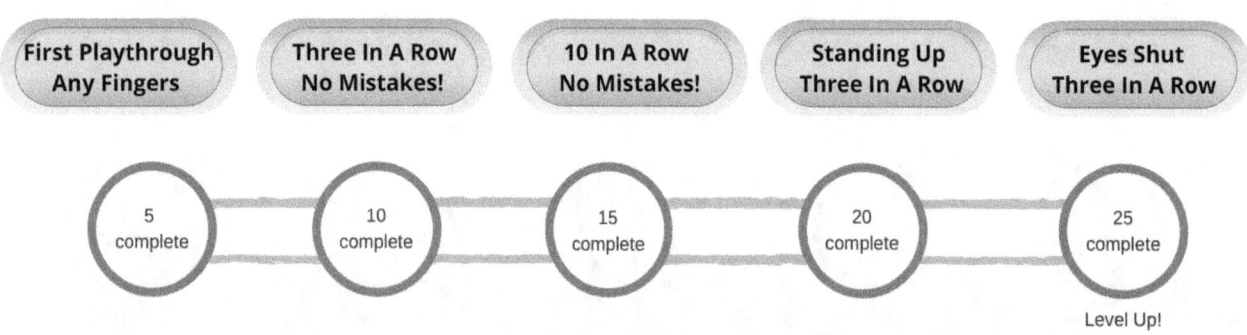

© Guitar Ninjas
The White Belt Book

Lesson 19 - Learning The Notes

In order to properly understand how the guitar works we need to know where all the notes are on the guitar fretboard. Fortunately, this is quite easy once you know the three special rules which make up our Note Memorisation Formula.

Note Memorisation Formula

Here are three rules that will help you work out the location of any note on any string provided you have a reference point to start from.

- The Musical Alphabet contains the notes A B C D E F & G. After the G note we go back to A and start over. Progress sequentially through the alphabet from your start point.
- The same note repeats every 12 frets. If E is 0, fret 12 will also be E.
- The notes 'E & F' and 'B & C' are buddy notes and will always be found immediately next to each other. Every other note has a 1 fret gap in between them.

You can use the Note Memorisation Formula to work out the notes along any string. In order to effectively use the Level-Up system which we'll learn about in the next section you will need to know the notes along strings 1, 3 & 6.

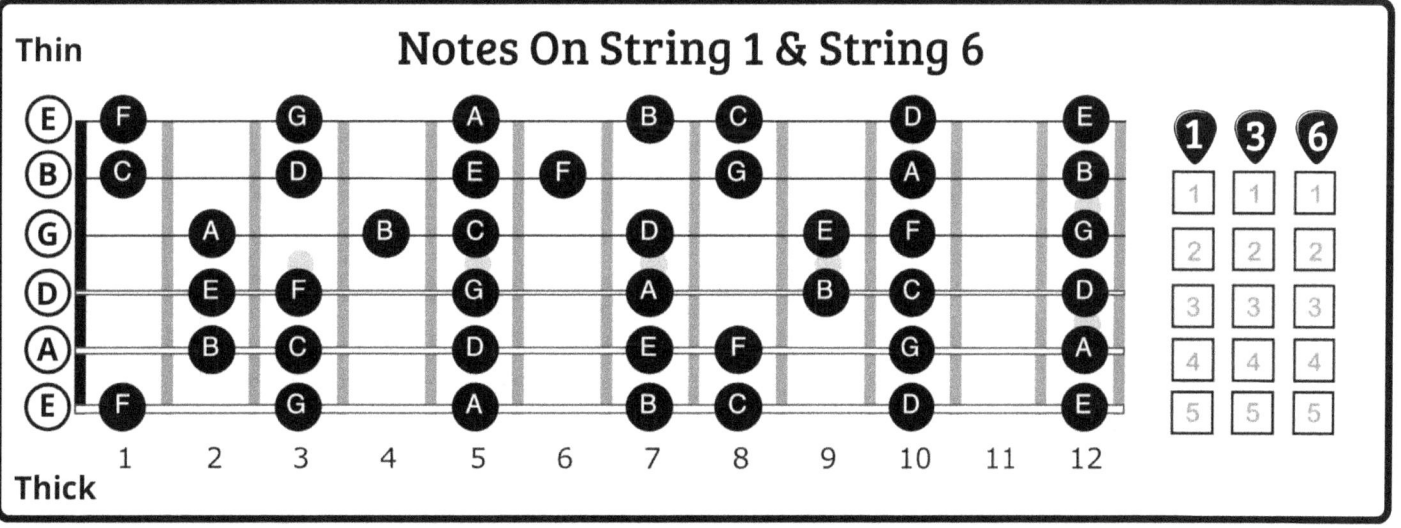

Tip: Strings 1 & 6 are both tuned to 'E' and will have the same notes at the same frets

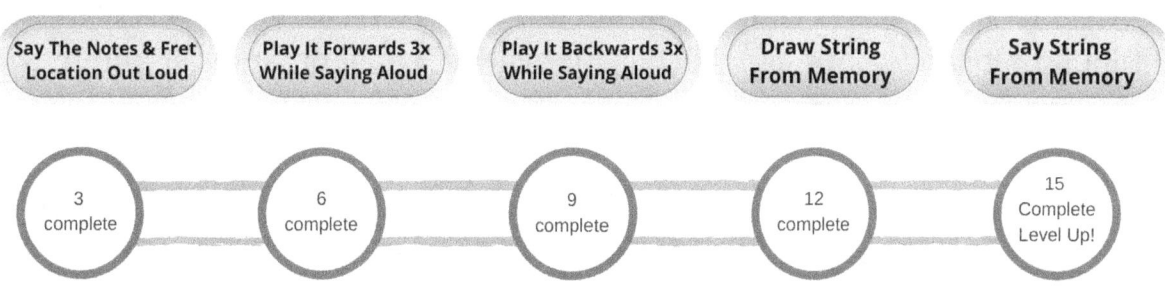

Part 2

The Level-Up System

Did you know that 90% of people who start learning how to play the guitar end up quitting within the first 12 months?

It's a staggering statistic that shows that something is wrong with the traditional approach to learning how to play guitar. While every other area of education has evolved over the last few decades, in most instances music lessons are taught the same way they were hundreds of years ago which is completely out of touch with the needs of modern students.

But fear not, we've got a solution! We've created a completely new approach to learning the guitar that will yield far better results. Instead of repeating the same old methods and expecting different outcomes (which we all know is the definition of insanity), our approach is innovative, efficient, and tailored to the needs of today's learners.

Say goodbye to overwhelm and frustration that leads to quitting early, and get ready to thrive on your guitar journey!

Lesson 20 - The Level Up System

When it comes to learning how to play the guitar, many of us start by trying to learn the chords we hear our favourite artists play on recordings.

However, this approach often leads to frustration as it can take 6-12 months just to learn and memorize the basic chord shapes, let alone smoothly transition between them while strumming complex rhythm patterns with your other hand.

The problem lies in our expectations. We tend to compare ourselves to our favourite artists who have years of practice under their belts, while we may have just started our guitar-playing journey a few weeks or months earlier. It's an unfair comparison that can lead to self-doubt and ultimately result in you quitting the guitar altogether.

Think about it this way - you wouldn't expect to be as good as Michael Jordan or LeBron James after just three weeks of basketball training, so why put that kind of pressure on yourself when learning guitar?

It's important to make peace with the fact that it takes time, typically 2-3 years, for most people to become truly comfortable with their guitar playing. Embrace the process, allow yourself to make mistakes, and don't be afraid to sound like a beginner during this time.

Remember, it's all part of the learning journey, and with dedication and patience, you'll get better and achieve your goals!

Most People Take The Wrong Approach To Learning Chords

When it comes to learning chords, many people take the wrong approach. Imagine if I were your personal trainer at the gym and tried to get you to do a 100kg (220lb) bench press on your very first day. There would be a 99.9% chance that you wouldn't be able to do it. No matter how hard you tried or how many attempts you took, you would only end up fatigued and frustrated with repeated failures.

It's clear that attempting to lift weights that are too heavy for us is a bad idea in the context of the gym. Yet, when it comes to learning guitar, we often dive right into

The Level-Up System

the deep end and try to play chords that are way beyond our level, only to get frustrated when we fail.

Trying to learn bar chords, for example, is like attempting to lift 100kg weights without working our way up to it. It's just not going to happen without several weeks or even months of practice.

Even "*standard*" open chords, which are found in every major beginner guitar book, are equivalent to lifting 80kg weights and require a lot of effort to work up to.

This unrealistic approach to learning chords results in many people quitting guitar prematurely because they lack the patience or discipline to stick with it for 6 months until the complex movements become required to play chords and transition between them smoothly (while strumming) become muscle memory.

But fear not, there is a better way, and I'm here to teach it to you!

Introducing The Level-Up Method

If we were in a gym and I was training you to do a 100kg (220lb) bench press, here is the process I would take:

- I would introduce you to the exercise with a broomstick and make sure you were doing everything correctly with 0% chance of failure or hurting yourself.
- Once you could perform the exercise correctly with no weight I would upgrade you to a light metal bar of 5-10kg
- Once you could perform the bench press correctly to a specific number of reps I would increase the difficulty by giving you a 20kg Olympic bar
- Over the next few weeks and months, we would gradually add additional weight plates and progressively increase the weight you were lifting and the number of reps you performed until you reached your goal of benching 100kg.

It might take us months or even years to get there, but as long as we consistently work towards our goal and put in the work required, we will eventually get there.

The Level-Up System

Applying This Approach To Guitar

You need to abandon any preconceived notion of what is the right way to learn guitar or what your playing should sound like at the beginner phase.

90% of people who start learning how to play the guitar quit in the first 12 months. I guarantee you that if you learn the same traditional way as everybody else then you'll end up with the same result - quitting!

So instead we're going to break guitar playing down into different levels and redefine what success looks like as a beginner guitarist and work our way up to more challenging levels as we gain more experience and develop more control and coordination of our fingers.

A levelled approach to learning guitar would look like this:

- Level 1 - Single Note Bass Lines
- Level 2 - Power Chords
- Level 3 - One Finger Triads
- Level 4 - Simplified Open Chords
- Level 5 - Standard Open Chords (this is where most people start and fail)
- Level 6 - Bar Chords

Most people start at level 5 or 6 with Open Chords or Bar Chords and wonder why they fail.

Instead, we can start at Level 1 and play along to an entire song using **One Finger** on one string with relatively little effort.

Then once we can do this comfortably we can make things more challenging and move on to Level 2 where we play the piece with **Power Chords**.

Then once we can do this the next step will be Level 3 where we use movable **One Finger Triads**.

Each time we level up it will sound more and more like the original recording until we work our way up to finally playing along using the same chords they do.

The Level-Up System

Climbing The Ladder

So far we've only talked about what our fretting hand will be doing when it comes to the different levels of chords that we can play on the guitar.

Part of what makes guitar challenging is that we have to coordinate two hands doing two very different movements at the same time.

If we try to co-ordinate switching between two chord shapes that we're not familiar with while simultaneously trying to strum a complex rhythm pattern with our other hand the result will be like most people's first attempt at driving a manual car - It's just way too much to think about all at once and completely overwhelming!

So just like our Strumming Hand had different levels of chords, so too our Picking Hand will have it's own levels for strumming and picking patterns. Here is a basic outline:

- Level 1 - One pick/strum per bar
- Level 2 - Four picks/strums per bar
- Level 3 - A simplified picking/strumming pattern
- Level 4 - The written picking/strumming pattern at a reduced speed
- Level 5 - The written picking/strumming pattern at speed

I like to use the analogy of a ladder for the Level-Up System because a ladder has two sides that relate to the two different roles our hands have when playing guitar.

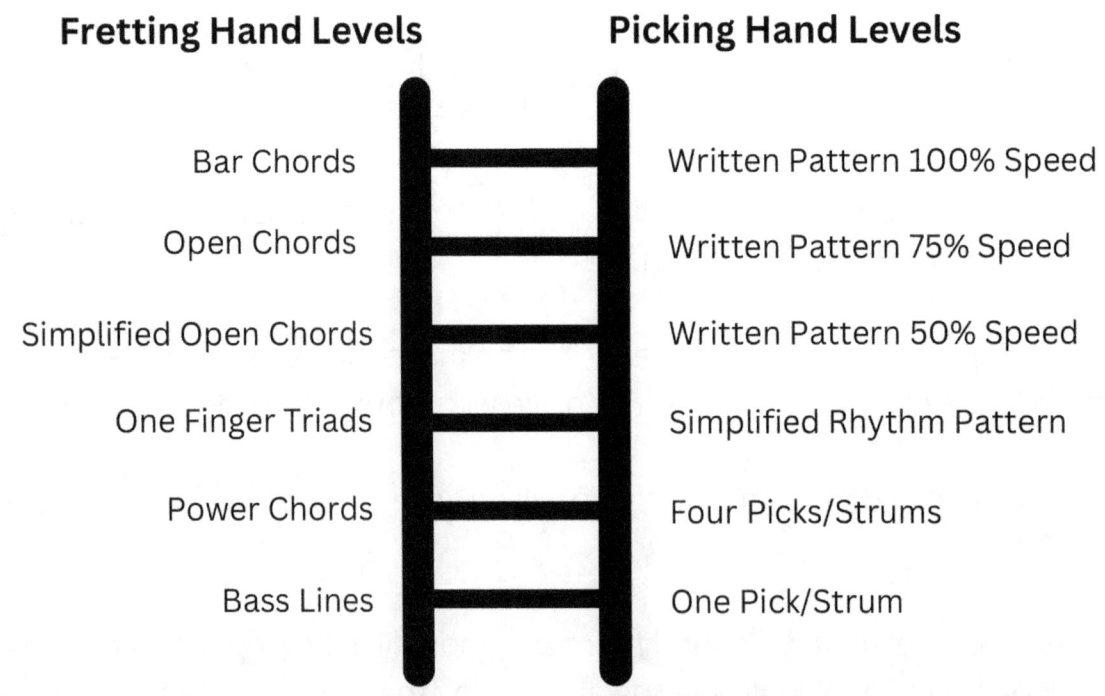

Fretting Hand Levels	Picking Hand Levels
Bar Chords	Written Pattern 100% Speed
Open Chords	Written Pattern 75% Speed
Simplified Open Chords	Written Pattern 50% Speed
One Finger Triads	Simplified Rhythm Pattern
Power Chords	Four Picks/Strums
Bass Lines	One Pick/Strum

Lesson 21 - Level 1 = One Finger, One String

If you know the names of the notes across string 6 then you know everything you need in order to play along to your favourite songs.

All you have to do is play the note that matches the name of the chord in time with the music. This is called '*playing the bassline*' and is what bass players do when playing in a band. It also happens to be Level 1 in the Level-Up system.

Playing the bassline will allow you to play along to any chord-based song straight away and is a great foundational level to start building our skills.

How To Play The Bass Line

You can play a bass line to any song by simply playing the note that matches the name of the chord on string 6 and letting it ring out for the duration of the bar. Let's take a look at the chord progression to *Knocking On Heaven's Door* below:

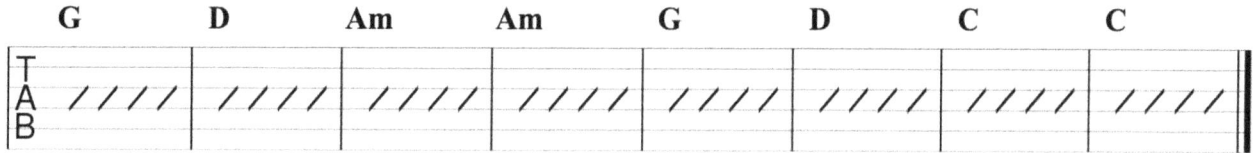

In Knocking On Heaven's Door, the chords are G D Am Am, then G D C C. In order to play along to the song you just find out which frets the notes G, D, A & C are located at and then play them in time with the music. Work out the fret locations from the diagram of string 6 below:

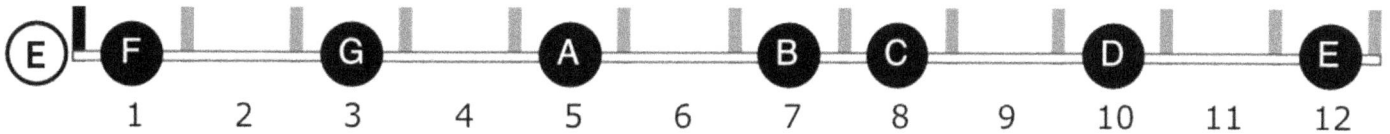

Hopefully, you figured out that G is found on fret 3, D is at fret 10, A is at fret 5 and C is fret 8. Therefore, to play the song you need only to play frets 3 10 5 5, then 3 10 8 8 in time with the music and you will be playing the bass line. It couldn't be easier! Here are the tabs below just incase!

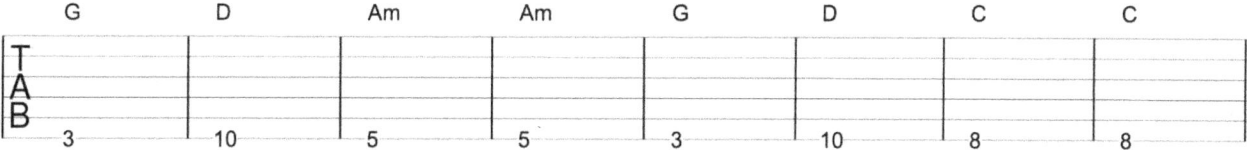

Lesson 22 - Level 2 = Power Chords

Power Chords are a special type of movable chord shape that can be substituted in place of any Major or Minor chord.

This means that instead of memorising a dozen different shapes and having to work at developing the muscle memory needed to change between them smoothly enough to sound musical, you can just memorise the Power Chord shape and move it along string 5 or 6 in place of any chord. Here are the Power Chord Shapes:

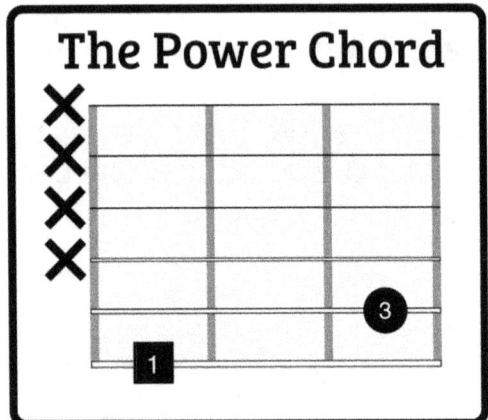 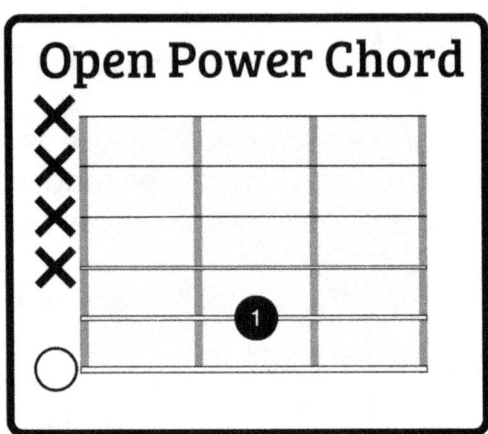

Power Chords take on the name of the note that they are played from.

To play the F Power Chord (written as F5) you put your first finger on the F note at fret 1 on string 6, and your third finger on the 5th string at the 3rd fret. Your third finger is always two frets higher on the string above your first finger. Below is a diagram of the notes along strings 5 & 6 to help you find where to play each chord.

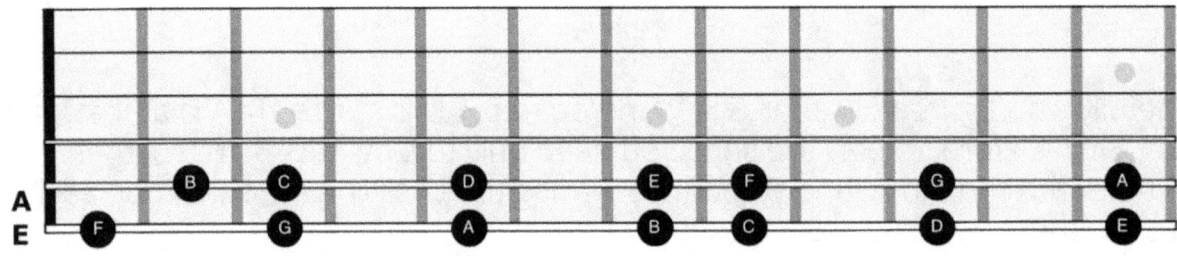

Here is Knocking On Heaven's Door using Power Chords:

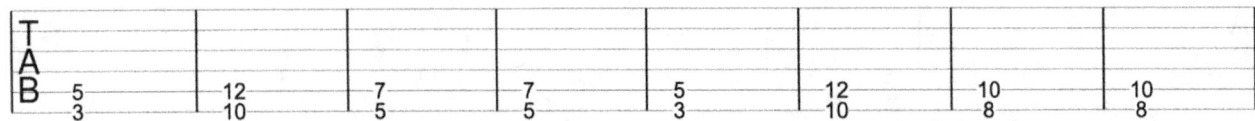

© Guitar Ninjas
The White Belt Book
www.GuitarNinjas.com.au

Lesson 23 - Level 3 = One Finger Triads

A Triad is the smallest form of a chord that contains just three notes. If you're learning how to play chords on a piano then you will start by learning triads.

For whatever reason, guitarists usually go straight to using 5 and 6 string open chords (which are far more challenging) and don't normally learn triads until much later on.

Level 3 in our Level-Up system introduces two triad shapes, a Minor Triad and a Major Triad, both of which can be played with just one finger!

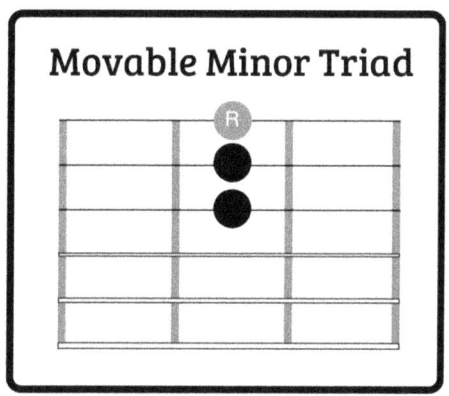
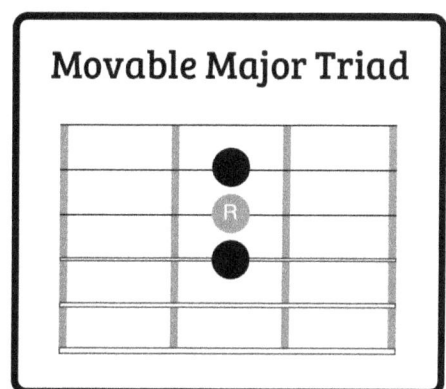

You can play any Minor Chord using the Movable Minor Triad Shape on the first three strings. Simply align your finger with the root note on String 1, bar it across the first three strings and strum. EG. If you want to play a G Minor Chord then play the shape at fret 3.

The Major chord works the exact same way except that you will use the shape on strings 2-4 instead. Line your finger up with the root note on string 3 and strum. Eg. If you want to play a D chord you will play the shape at fret 7 but strum strings 2, 3 & 4. The notes along strings 1 and 3 are given below as a reference. (note that the open position works too).

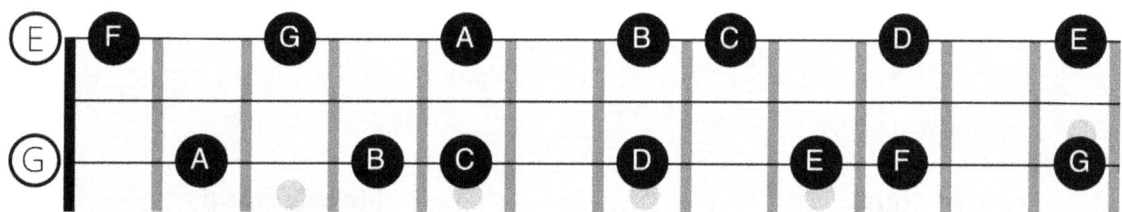

Here is Knocking On Heaven's Door using One Finger Movable Triads

```
    G        D        Am       Am        G        D        C        C
                      5        5
T—0——————7————————5————————5————————0————————7————————3————————3———
A—0——————7————————5————————5————————0————————7————————3————————3———
B—0——————7————————5————————5————————0————————7————————3————————3———
```

© Guitar Ninjas
The White Belt Book
www.GuitarNinjas.com.au

Lesson 24 - Chord Progressions

A **Chord Progression** is when you play two or more chords one after the other. Most songs are simply chord progressions with singing over the top of them.

A chord progression will generally be notated as follows:

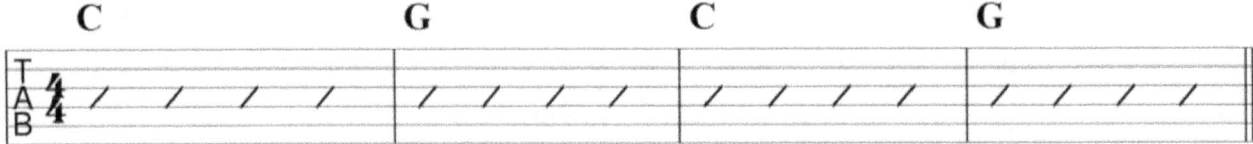

You can see that you need to play a C chord in the first bar, and a G chord in the second bar, another C chord in the 3rd bar and a G chord in the fourth bar.

The dashes are used to signal strums. If you see / / / / you need to strum four times on each chord before changing to the new chord.

How To Play Chord Progressions

- Put your fingers in the right place for the C chord.
- Strum four times.
- Put your fingers in the right place for the G chord.
- Strum four times.
- Repeat this over and over for 20 repetitions, or one minute, whichever comes first.

How To Play Chord Progressions Using The Level-Up System

As stated earlier it's going to take months to get comfortable with traditional chord changes. Instead of making your life difficult, we'll instead be focusing on playing chord progressions in three levels:

Fretting Hand

- Level 1 - Bass Lines
- Level 2 - Power Chords
- Level 3 - One Finger Triads

Picking Hand

- Level 1 - One Pick/Strum
- Level 2 - Four Picks/Strums
- Level 3 - Simple Pattern

Once you get comfortable with these three levels you can explore additional chords found in your Guitar Workbook 1.

Lesson 25 - Levelled Chord Progressions

Over the next few pages, we're going to take you through 10 of the most common chord progressions used in contemporary guitar music and pop songs.

Each progression will be presented in the key of G Major with three levels for you to work through.

The sooner you memorise your chord shapes and develop the ability to change between them smoothly, the sooner you can play along to real songs. Practising these chord progressions will prepare you for playing your favourite tunes.

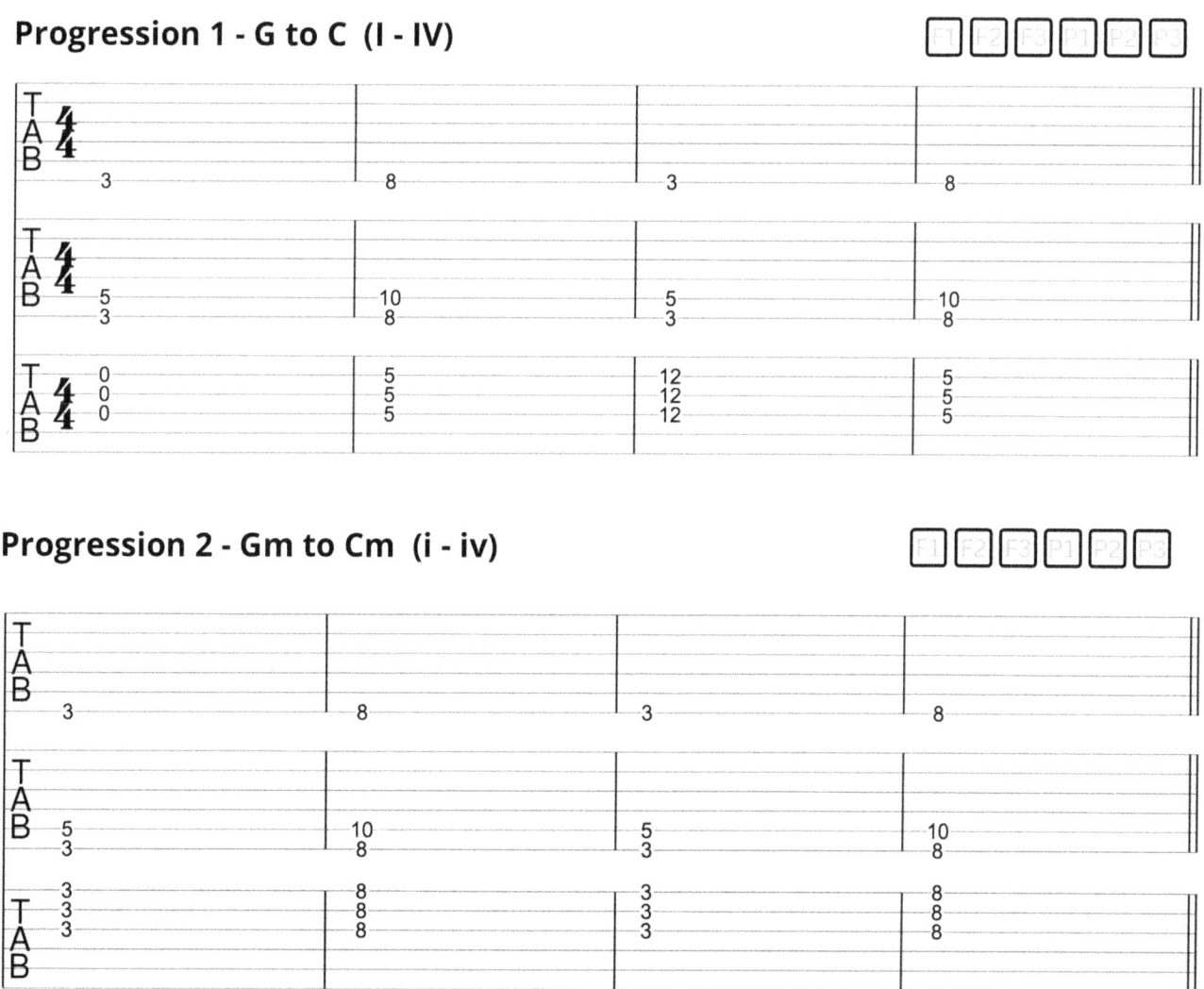

Tip: Play the progression 3x in a row without a mistake at level 1 before moving on to the next level. You can use the checkboxes to keep track of which level you are up to with each hand.

Levelled Chord Progressions

Progression 3 - G to D (I - V)   ☐F1 ☐F2 ☐F3 ☐P1 ☐P2 ☐P3

```
T|--------------|--------------|--------------|--------------||
A|--3-----------|--10----------|--3-----------|--10----------||
B|--------------|--------------|--------------|--------------||

T|--------------|--------------|--------------|--------------||
A|--5-----------|--12----------|--5-----------|--12----------||
B|--3-----------|--10----------|--3-----------|--10----------||

T|--0-----------|--7-----------|--12----------|--7-----------||
A|--0-----------|--7-----------|--12----------|--7-----------||
B|--0-----------|--7-----------|--12----------|--7-----------||
```

Progression 4 - Gm to Dm (i - v)   ☐F1 ☐F2 ☐F3 ☐P1 ☐P2 ☐P3

```
T|--------------|--------------|--------------|--------------||
A|--3-----------|--10----------|--3-----------|--10----------||
B|--------------|--------------|--------------|--------------||

T|--------------|--------------|--------------|--------------||
A|--5-----------|--12----------|--5-----------|--12----------||
B|--3-----------|--10----------|--3-----------|--10----------||

T|--3-----------|--7-----------|--3-----------|--7-----------||
A|--3-----------|--7-----------|--3-----------|--7-----------||
B|--3-----------|--7-----------|--3-----------|--7-----------||
```

Progression 5 - G to C to D to G (I - IV - V - I)   ☐F1 ☐F2 ☐F3 ☐P1 ☐P2 ☐P3

```
T|--------------|--------------|--------------|--------------||
A|--3-----------|--8-----------|--10----------|--3-----------||
B|--------------|--------------|--------------|--------------||

T|--------------|--------------|--------------|--------------||
A|--5-----------|--10----------|--12----------|--5-----------||
B|--3-----------|--8-----------|--10----------|--3-----------||

T|--0-----------|--5-----------|--7-----------|--12----------||
A|--0-----------|--5-----------|--7-----------|--12----------||
B|--0-----------|--5-----------|--7-----------|--12----------||
```

© Guitar Ninjas
The White Belt Book

Levelled Chord Progressions

Progression 6 - Gm to Cm to D to Gm (i - iv - V - i)

```
T|------------|------------|------------|------------||
A|--3---------|--8---------|-10---------|--3---------||
B|------------|------------|------------|------------||

T|------------|------------|------------|------------||
A|--5---------|-10---------|-12---------|--5---------||
B|--3---------|--8---------|-10---------|--3---------||

T|--3---------|--8---------|------------|--3---------||
A|--3---------|--8---------|--7---------|--3---------||
B|--3---------|--8---------|--7---------|--3---------||
                            --7---------
```

Progression 7 - G to C to D to C (I - IV - V - IV)

```
T|------------|------------|------------|------------||
A|--3---------|--8---------|-10---------|--8---------||
B|------------|------------|------------|------------||

T|------------|------------|------------|------------||
A|--5---------|-10---------|-12---------|-10---------||
B|--3---------|--8---------|-10---------|--8---------||

T|--0---------|--5---------|--7---------|--5---------||
A|--0---------|--5---------|--7---------|--5---------||
B|--0---------|--5---------|--7---------|--5---------||
```

Progression 8 - G to C to Em to D to G (I - IV - vi - V)

```
T|------------|------------|------------|------------||
A|--3---------|-10---------|--0---------|--8---------||
B|------------|------------|------------|------------||

T|------------|------------|------------|------------||
A|--5---------|-12---------|--2---------|-10---------||
B|--3---------|-10---------|--0---------|--8---------||

T|--0---------|--7---------|--0---------|--5---------||
A|--0---------|--7---------|--0---------|--5---------||
B|--0---------|--7---------|--0---------|--5---------||
```

Levelled Chord Progressions

Progression 9 - G to Em to C to D (I - vi - IV - V)   F1 F2 F3 P1 P2 P3

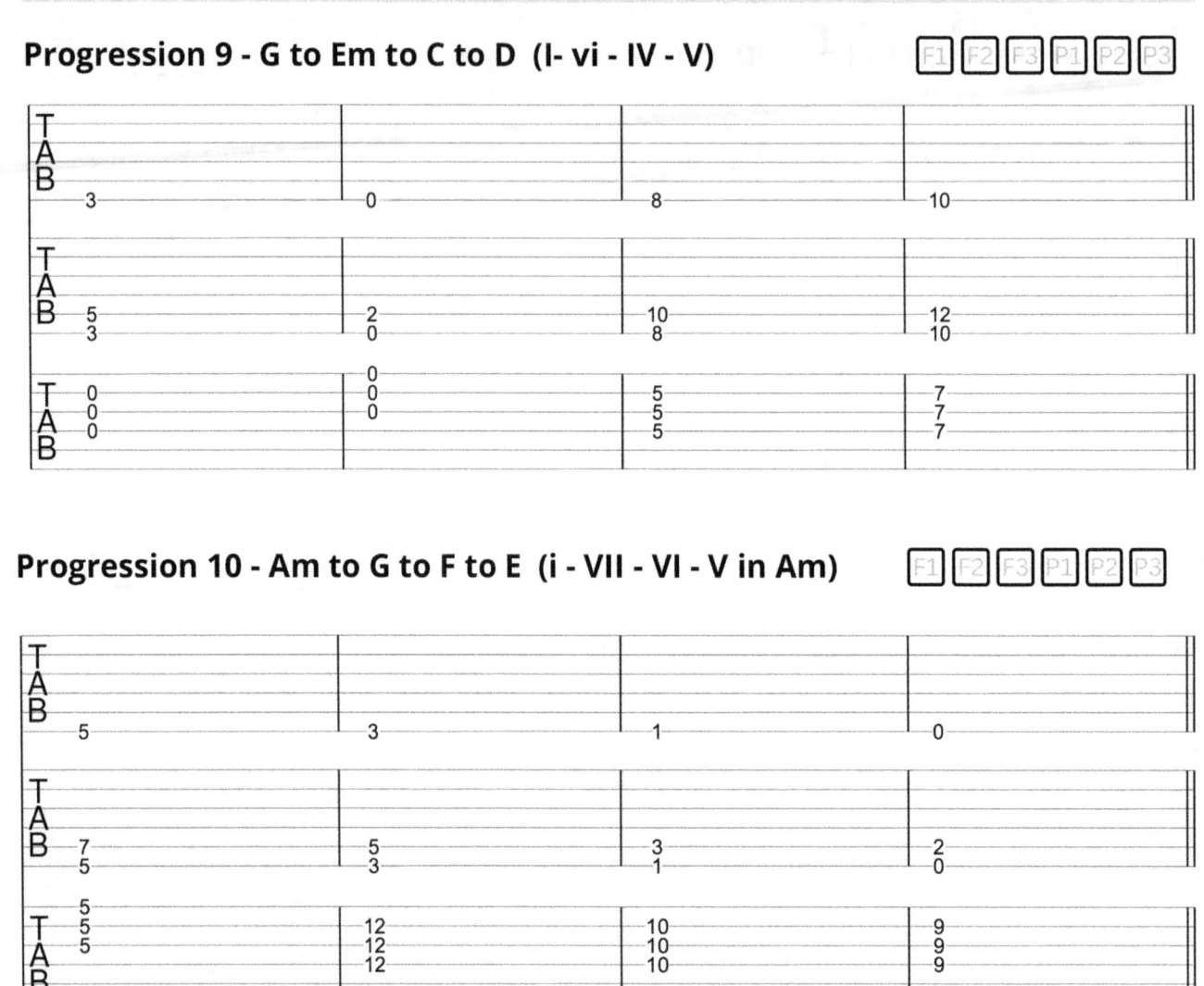

Progression 10 - Am to G to F to E (i - VII - VI - V in Am)   F1 F2 F3 P1 P2 P3

Taking It To The Next Level

Once you start getting the hang of the One Finger Triads you can begin exploring higher levels in your Guitar Workbook 1. Think of the Level 1 Beginner Chords on page 10 as being the 4th level for your fretting hand and continue from there.

- Additional Chords can be found from page 10 onwards
- Additional Chord Progressions can be found from pg 21 onwards
- Additional Strumming Patterns can be found on pages 27 onwards

You **do not** need to complete the entire White Belt Book before you start these additional levels. You can move onto them as soon as the One Finger Triad shapes become easy for you to use.

Bonus Lesson - The Four Chord Progression

There is a very special chord progression known as the Four Chord Progression that is used in thousands and thousands of songs!

It used the chords C, G, Am & F.

We've given you an overview of how to play the Four Chord Progression in seven levels from Bassline all the way up to Barre Chords.

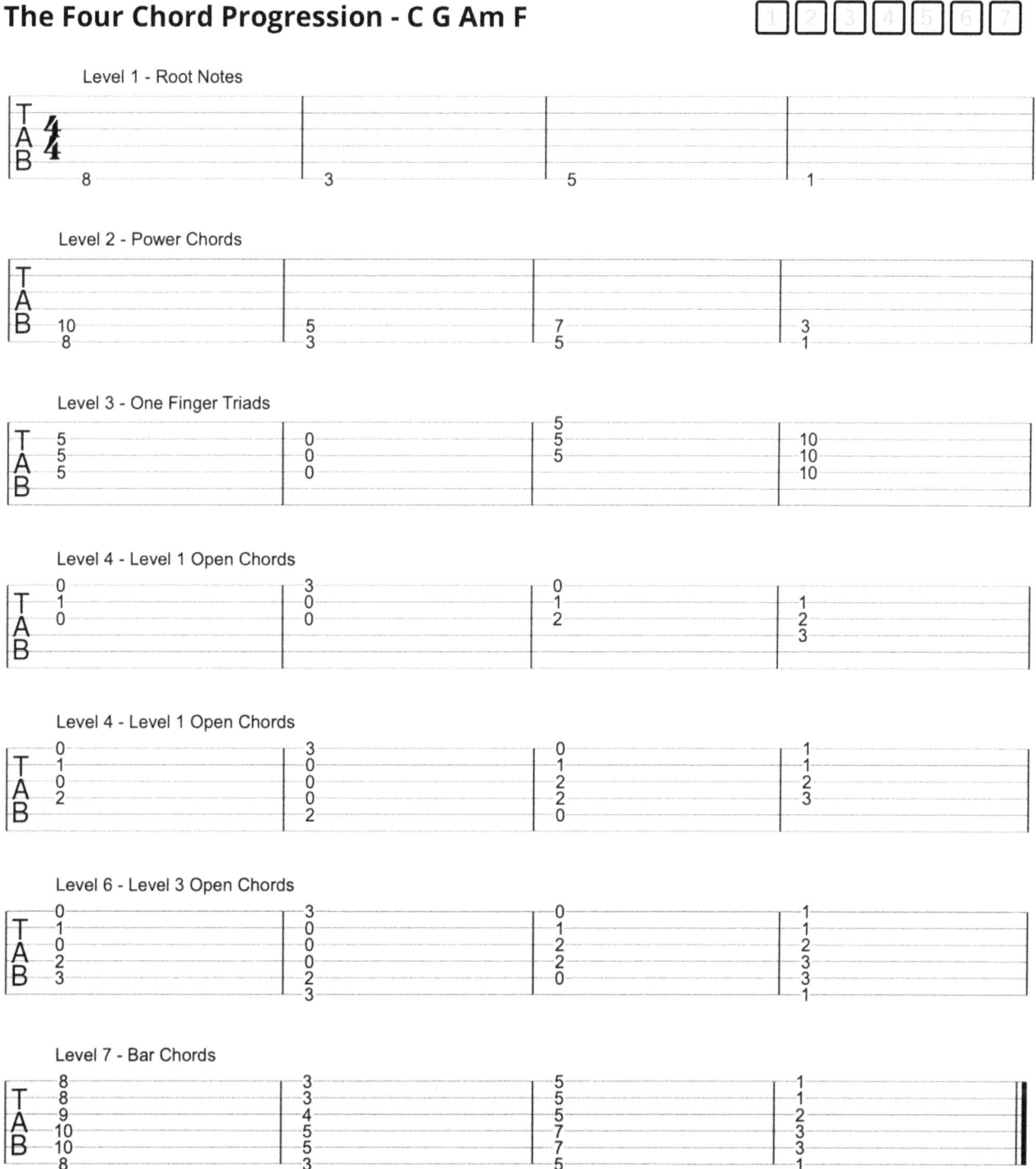

How To Tune Your Guitar

Having your guitar in tune will be very important whether you play on your own or with other people.

To tune a guitar all you need to do is pick the string and then turn the tuning peg that matches that string.

Now in order for the guitar to be in tune, each string has to match a particular pitch.

I like to say the phrase **E**aster **B**unnies **G**o **D**ancing **A**t **E**aster.

The first letter of each word becomes the name of the string, and the note we need to tune to.

- The first string is tuned to an E note (thinnest string)
- The second string is tuned to a B note
- The third string is tuned to an G note
- The fourth string is tuned to a D note
- The fifth string is tuned to an A note
- The sixth string is also tuned to an E note. (thickest string)

Most tuners these days will simply give you the name of the string you are playing and tell you whether you are sharp or flat. If you are really out of tune however, you may need to give the string a big twist in order to put it back into the right territory.

EG If you are tuning the E string but your tuner is showing you a B note, you need to tighten the string so it goes from B to C to D and then to E.

© Guitar Ninjas
The White Belt Book

Guitar Ninjas Practice Log

Name: _____   Month: _____

Date of Day 1 = _____   Date of Day 30/31 = _____

Practice Area	1	2	3	4	5	6	7	8	9	10	11	12	13	14	15	16	17	18	19	20	21	22	23	24	25	26	27	28	29	30	31
Study Pieces																															
Warmups																															
Scales																															
Melodies																															
Riffs																															
Chord Memorisation																															
Chord Progressions																															
Strumming Patterns																															
Rhythms																															
Note Memorisation																															
Songs & Repertoire																															

How To Use

Easy: Cross off the box that matches each practice item you worked on for that day.

Advanced: Write the number of minutes you practiced each item for in

- 3 Days In A Row → 1 complete
- 10 Days In A Row → 2 complete
- 15 Days In A Row → 3 complete
- Practice On 20 Or More Days → 4 complete
- Every Day Of The Month → 5 Complete Special Prize!

© Guitar Ninjas
The White Belt Book
www.GuitarNinjas.com.au

Summary

Congratulations! You have now completed the White Belt Book and have not only learned all the basic skills and concepts that you need to start playing guitar confidently but have also earned your White Belt!

To summarise what you have learned:

- Your fundamental guitar skills including picking, fretting & strumming.
- How to play along to any song using the Level-Up System.
- Some real guitar riffs and everything you need to practice effectively.

You are now ready to take it to the next level of your guitar-playing journey.

What You Should Do Next

Continue your guitar playing journey with the next level of Guitar Ninjas. Choose between face to face lessons at one of our studio locations or Online Zoom lessons from the comfort of your own home. Both types of lessons are taught by a member of our professional team of teachers to ensure you get the highest quality lessons anywhere in the world no matter where you are.

Want to experience an online guitar lesson program like no other? Continue your guitar playing journey with us at *Guitar Dojo Online* - an virtual guitar university with over 700 videos and 40 courses as well as practice tracking, daily challenges and our Guitar Ninja Ascension System to take you from where you are now to a Black Belt Level Guitar Ninja!

About The Author

Michael Gumley is a professional guitar teacher, author and musical educator from Melbourne, Australia. He is the founder of Guitar Ninjas, Melbourne Guitar Academy and The Guitar Dojo Online Virtual Guitar Academy.

Michael began playing guitar at the age of 15 when his cousin showed him a few riffs. It was like getting hit by a bolt of lightning and he knew from the very first note he played that guitar was what he wanted to do for the rest of his life. Michael would go on to practice up to 6 hours a day throughout high school in the hopes of becoming the world's next guitar hero so that he could join his own heroes Eddie Van Halen, Slash and Yngwie Malmsteen in the halls of eternal guitar glory.

Michael played in both cover and original bands while studying a Bachelor Degree in Music Performance and took lessons from some of Melbourne's best teachers. He also began attending guitar playing events and teaching summits in the USA as his passion for guitar led him to pursue a full time teaching career.

At the age of 25 he took the plunge and decided to commit to music full time. After quitting his "day job" as a checkout assistant at the local supermarket, he founded Melbourne Guitar Academy and has never looked back. He is currently on the artist roster for Ormsby Guitars, Line 6 FX & Ernie Ball Strings, and has had past endorsement deals with ESP Guitars, Blackstar Amplification & Dean Markley Strings.

Michael looks to share his love of guitar & passion for music with each and every one of his students, and can't wait to help you with your guitar playing. You can email Michael at info@GuitarNinjas.com.au or by following him on social media with the tag @MichaelGumley

Learning Is So Much Easier With Guitar Dojo Online

Instantly Access The Accompanying White Belt Online Course Taught Directly By Author and Expert Teacher Michael Gumley

Get direct guidance from the author of The White Belt Book as he demonstrates every skill, concept, technique, challenge and worksheet with over 2 hours of high definition video footage. It's the next best thing to being in a live lesson with the added advantage that you can access it any time, anywhere in the world as you need it.

- Get step by step guidance through every topic in the book.
- Look and listen to every example as it's demonstrated to you.
- Get great learning insights and additional commentary that couldn't be fit onto the pages of this book.
- Join a community of other Guitar Ninjas from all around the world!

All Journeys Are Made Easier With An Expert Guide

Who Better To Guide You Than The One Who Wrote The Book? Sign up for Guitar Ninjas At The Link Below!

www.GuitarNinjas.com.au